BEES
BUILD
BEEHIVES

BY ELIZABETH RAUM   ILLUSTRATED BY ROMINA MARTÍ

AMICUS ILLUSTRATED and AMICUS INK are published by Amicus
P.O. Box 1329, Mankato, MN 56002
www.amicuspublishing.us

LIBRARY OF CONGRESS CATALOGING-IN-PUBLICATION DATA
Names: Raum, Elizabeth, author. | Martí, Romina, illustrator.
Title: Bees build beehives / by Elizabeth Raum ; illustrated by Romina Martí.
Description: Mankato, Minnesota : Amicus Illustrated, [2018] | Series: Animal
    builders | Audience: K to grade 3.
Identifiers: LCCN 2016049820 (print) | LCCN 2017003639 (ebook) | ISBN
    9781681511696 (library binding) | ISBN 9781681521503 (paperback) |
    ISBN 9781681512594 (e-book)
Subjects: LCSH: Bees—Juvenile literature. | Beehives—Juvenile literature.
Classification: LCC QL565.2 .R39 2017 (print) | LCC QL565.2 (ebook) | DDC
    595.79/9—dc23
LC record available at https://lccn.loc.gov/2016049820

EDITOR: Rebecca Glaser
DESIGNER: Kathleen Petelinsek

Printed in the United States of America
HC 10 9 8 7 6 5 4 3 2 1
PB 10 9 8 7 6 5 4 3 2 1

ABOUT THE AUTHOR

As a child, Elizabeth Raum hiked through the Vermont woods searching for signs that animals lived nearby. She read every animal book in the school library. She now lives in North Dakota and writes books for young readers. Many of her books are about animals. To learn more, go to: www.elizabethraum.net.

ABOUT THE ILLUSTRATOR

Romina Martí is an illustrator who lives and works in Barcelona, Spain, where her ideas come to life for all audiences. She loves to discover and draw all kinds of creatures from around the planet, who then become the main characters for the majority of her work. To learn more, go to: rominamarti.com

A honeybee flies into the hollow of an old tree. Is the hole big enough for a hive? Yes. It looks perfect.

The old hive was too crowded. The queen and thousands of workers left to find a new home.

The honeybee returns to the swarm. She does a waggle dance. It tells the other bees how to find the hollow tree.

Other scouts check it out. It looks good. The swarm flies to the new hollow. It will take about 45 days to build the new hive.

First, they make wax. The bees' bodies can do this.
Then they chew the wax to make it soft.

The bees build tiny six-sided cells out of wax. A figure with six sides is called a hexagon. The hexagons fit together to form a honeycomb. The bees fill every crack with a mix of tree resin, pollen, and honey.

The new hive will need a lot more bees. The queen bee finds a drone, or male bee. They mate. The drone dies after mating.

The queen bee lays 1,500 to 3,000 eggs a day.
There will be a lot of baby bees in the hive!

The queen puts one egg in each cell. Three days later, the eggs hatch. The cells are the perfect place for the larvae to grow up.

Nurse bees feed the larvae pollen and nectar until they enter the pupa stage. When the pupas turn into adults, they help take care of the hive.

There are many jobs to do inside the hive. New adults clean the hive. They feed the larvae. They make wax and build new cells. No wonder we call them busy bees!

16

Many animals attack the hive. Bears try to steal the honey. Skunks, frogs, lizards, spiders, and other bugs try to eat the bees. Guard bees protect the hive. BUZZ! STING!

But bees don't stay in the hive all the time. They have plenty of work to do outside the hive, too. Worker bees collect pollen and nectar to bring back for making honey.

Drops of pollen stick to a bee's hairy body. They carry
pollen from one flower to the next. When the pollen mixes
together, plants grow fruits and vegetables. Thanks, bees!

When winter sets in, the bees stay in the hive. They eat
the honey and pollen they stored during summer and fall.

Once again, the hive is crowded. A new queen hatches. The old queen and half the workers form a swarm. It's time to build a new hive.

Where Honey Bees Live

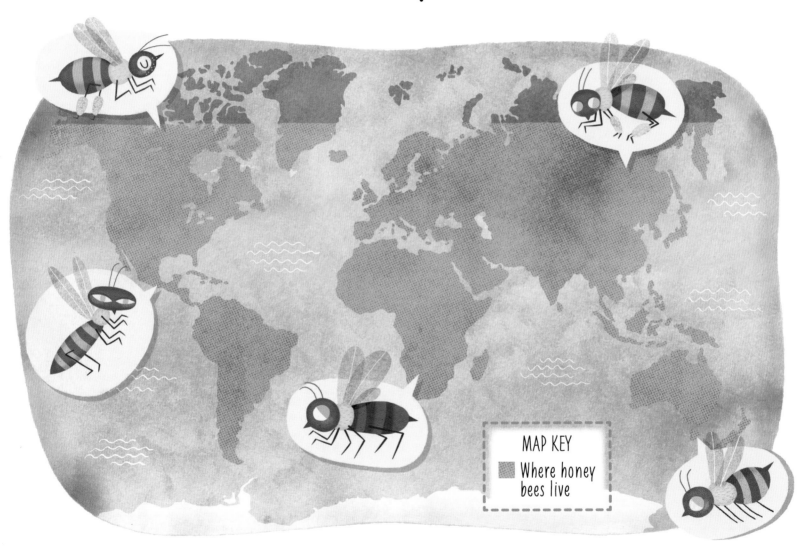

MAP KEY

Where honey bees live

Build Like a Bee

Bees build their hives with many repeated hexagons because it is a strong shape. Build with paper to see how hexagons fit together.

WHAT BEES USE	WHAT YOU NEED
Beeswax	Construction paper
Tree resin and pollen	Glue stick
Instinct	Ruler

WHAT YOU DO

1. Cut construction paper into strips 1 inch (2.5 cm) wide by 7 inches (17.5 cm) long.

2. Use a ruler to mark each strip every 1 inch (2.5 cm).

3. Fold the strips along the marks to make hexagons. The last section overlaps with the first one. Use a glue stick to glue the sections together.

4. Fit the hexagons beside one another and glue them together. They should fit perfectly! Now imagine hundreds more, but much smaller. This is what the inside of a beehive looks like.

GLOSSARY

drone A male honeybee with no stinger; its job is to mate with the queen bee.

honeycomb The rows of cells in a beehive that are used to store honey, pollen, and eggs.

larvae Baby insects between the stage of egg and pupa; larvae look like worms.

mate To join together to make young.

nectar A sweet juice that comes from plants; used to make honey.

pollen A fine yellow powder produced by plants, needed to make seeds.

pupa An insect in an inactive stage of development between a larva and an adult.

queen A female bee in a hive that lays eggs; she is the largest bee.

resin A sticky substance that comes from trees.

swarm A group of honey bees that leave the hive together to build a new hive.

worker A female bee that performs one of the many jobs in the hive, from cleaning and taking care of babies, to building honeycomb and gathering nectar and pollen.

READ MORE

Ang, Karen. *Inside the Bees' Hive*. New York, N.Y.: Bearport Pub., 2014.

Chrustowski, Rick. *Bee Dance*. New York, N.Y.: Henry Holt and Company, 2015.

Sullivan, Martha. *If You Love Honey: Nature's Connections*. Nevada City, Calif.: Dawn Publications, 2015.

WEBSITES

Bee Facts for Kids
http://kids.sandiegozoo.org/animals/insects/bee
See pictures of bees and learn some basic bee facts.

Honeybee: National Geographic Kids
http://kids.nationalgeographic.com/animals/honeybee
View photos and learn about bee behavior in hives, plus compare their speed and size.

World's Weirdest: Honey Bee Dance Moves
http://video.nationalgeographic.com/video/weirdest-bees-dance
Watch a honey bee do a waggle dance to tell other bees where pollen is.

Every effort has been made to ensure that these websites are appropriate for children. However, because of the nature of the Internet, it is impossible to guarantee that these sites will remain active indefinitely or that their contents will not be altered.